D1631846

The Power of the BR Standard 2-6-0s

A delightful branch-line scene featuring Class 2MT No 78048 ready to leave Coldstream station with the single-coach 9.56am Berwick upon Tweed–St Boswells on 1 June 1962. The locomotive went new to Edinburgh St Margarets shed and after around five years moved to Hawick, where it was to spend the rest of its career, which ended in July 1964. *M. Mensing*

Class 4MT No 76001 was transferred from Motherwell to Fort William in June 1960 to help out on the Mallaig line and stayed for two years before moving to Corkerhill in Glasgow. It is shown at Glenfinnan, the train being the 3.15pm from Fort William on 13 August 1960. With two vans and six coaches behind the tender the locomotive put in an excellent performance, gaining six minutes on the schedule and although driven hard on the banks was never shy for steam. The author was travelling on the footplate, and the ride was very much better than on the run-down Class K1 on which he returned. *Gavin Morrison*

The Power of the
BR Standard 2-6-0s

Gavin Morrison

An imprint of
Ian Allan Publishing

Contents

First published 2006

ISBN (10) 0 86093 589 2
ISBN (13) 978 0 86093 589 6

All rights reserved. No part of this book may be reproduced or transmitted in any form or by any means, electronic or mechanical, including photocopying, recording or by any information storage and retrieval system, without permission from the Publisher in writing.

© Ian Allan Publishing Ltd 2006

Published by Ian Allan Publishing

an imprint of Ian Allan Publishing Ltd, Hersham, Surrey KT12 4RG
Printed in England by Ian Allan Printing Ltd, Hersham, Surrey KT12 4RG

Code: 0604/A3

Visit the Ian Allan Publishing website at www.ianallanpublishing.com

Introduction

Designed by BR Chief Mechanical Engineer Robert A. Riddles, the Standard Class 4MT ('76xxx') and 2MT ('78xxx') 2-6-0s were little more than Ivatt Class 4MT and 2MT 2–6–0s with minor modifications, lessons having been learned from the mistakes made with the draughting of the Ivatt '4MTs' and their double chimneys (earning them their 'Doodlebug' nickname).

The first batch of '4MTs' (Nos 76000-19) were built at Horwich and delivered to the Scottish and Southern regions between December 1952 and July 1953, whilst Doncaster produced Nos 76020-4 for the North Eastern Region during December 1952 and January 1953. The class eventually numbered 115 locomotives, No 76114 being the last new steam locomotive to be built at Doncaster Works, in October 1959. In the meantime the cost of construction increased from £16,892 to £20,577 per locomotive. The type was the seventh BR design, with two cylinders (as were all the BR Standards with the exception of No 71000 *Duke of Gloucester*), and 225lb/sq in boiler pressure. With 5ft 3in driving wheels, they were intended as freight locomotives, but it was quickly realised that they rode well and were perfectly suitable for passenger duties, hence the '4MT' (Mixed Traffic) classification. Visually the class varied hardly at all, except for Nos 76053-69, which were attached to the BR1B tenders, increasing their water capacity to 4,725 gallons (and coal capacity to 7 tons) for working on the Southern Region, which lacked water troughs.

All regions except the Western received new members of the class, which were allocated as far north as Blair Atholl and Fort William and as far south as Bournemouth. They were well received everywhere, due to their performance and ease of maintenance, as well as a high degree of comfort for crews. The Southern Region in particular used them on passenger work, and in the summer months they were used on expresses between Waterloo and Lymington Pier, taking over from 'Schools' 4-4-0s, as larger locomotives would not fit on the turntable at Brockenhurst. They were also used extensively on the Somerset & Dorset line, both as pilots and as train engines. The famous Stainmore route over the Pennines was another line on which they were regular performers.

Title page:
To mark the closure of the Stainmore line the North Eastern branch of the Railway Correspondence & Travel Society (RCTS) organised the 'Stainmore Limited' farewell tour on 20 January 1962. Headed by well-cleaned '3MT' No 77003 and '4MT' No 76049, the special — the last westbound train over the line — is seen leaving Kirkby Stephen East for Tebay. *Gavin Morrison*

A few members of the class lasted for around 15 years, whereas some survived for only nine, due to line closures and the rapid spread of 'dieselisation'. The first (No 76028) was withdrawn in May 1964, while the last batch went in December 1967. Fortunately four locomotives — Nos 76017, 76077, 76079 and 76084 — survive in preservation, No 76079 travelling widely over Network Rail and putting in some spectacular performances.

Looking back on the building programme for the BR Standard designs, it is difficult to understand why so many locomotives were built, and why the Class 3MT ('77xxx') locomotives were built at all. The original order for the latter was for 25 locomotives to be built at Swindon, but the last five (Nos 77020-4) were cancelled in September 1956. The first five appeared between February and March 1954 and went to the North Eastern Region, and the last (No 77019) was completed by September 1954. Ten went to Scotland, where they remained allocated mainly around the Glasgow and Hurlford areas, and the other 10 went to the North Eastern Region, where they were frequently transferred between sheds; however, No 77011 was ultimately withdrawn from Northwich, on the London Midland Region, while No 77014 escaped in 1966 to Guildford, on the Southern Region, where it worked for 16 months and became the last of the class in service.

Again, it appears that the '3MTs' were well liked by the crews for their ease of maintenance and comfort and were fine on light branch-line passenger work and pick-up goods, but with the BR Type 6 200lb/sq in boiler they were under-powered and did not steam well when driven hard on routes such as the Stainmore line. Many of the North Eastern-allocated locomotives finished up at Stourton shed in Leeds, where they replaced Fowler 0-6-0s on local freights, whilst the Scottish examples apparently did little work. They would have been ideal locomotives for many preserved lines, but unfortunately none was preserved, the class being thus consigned to history.

Above:
Class 4MT, introduced December 1952; 115 built, all withdrawn by December 1967. *Ian Allan Library*

Left:
Class 3MT, introduced February 1954; 20 built, all withdrawn by July 1967. *Ian Allan Library*

The BR Class 2MT 2-6-0s were numbered 78000-64. All were constructed at Darlington Works between December 1952 and June 1956. They were virtually identical to the Ivatt Class 2MT 2-6-0s; indeed, the last Ivatts were still being delivered by Swindon Works as the first '78xxx' locomotives were emerging from Darlington. Cost per locomotive rose from £14,377 to £16,871 over the construction period. The boiler was the BR8, with a working pressure of 200lb/sq in, all the benefits gained from the draughting experiments with the Ivatt '2MTs' being incorporated, together with all the modern features for maintenance and crew comfort, producing fine machines which performed well and ran high mileages between overhauls.

The Southern and Eastern regions received no new Standard '2MTs', but during their working lives these locomotives were nevertheless allocated as far north as Fraserburgh and as far south as Willesden. Along with the Ivatt 2-6-0s they largely allowed the old branch-line classes to be withdrawn, but, as with many of the smaller BR Standard types, the work for which they were designed rapidly vanished, either through branch-line closures or due to the introduction of DMUs and Type 2 diesel locomotives. Gradually they were relegated to empty-stock duties and shunting, most ending up on the London Midland Region.

Externally there were no differences of note, the livery being lined black, with the usual exception of the Western Region, which painted most (if not all) of its allocation in lined or unlined green livery. Their cabside numbers varied in size depending on where they were overhauled. The '2MTs' are perhaps best remembered for their work on the Stainmore line, where they were highly regarded, as well as on the Cambrian and Mid-Wales routes, and not forgetting their rather easier branch-line duties in the Scottish Borders. As with other BR Standard classes, probably too many were built; despite being good performers and far superior to the locomotives they replaced, all were withdrawn long before they could justify their construction. No 78015 lasted only until November 1963, not quite managing 10 years of service, while the final survivors succumbed in May 1967.

Above:
Class 2MT, introduced December 1952; 55 built, all withdrawn by May 1967. *Ian Allan Library*

Four of the class passed into preservation, Nos 78022 and 78019 having been returned to working order, whilst No 78059 is to be converted to a 2-6-2T. No 78022 was fitted with a Giesl ejector by the Keighley & Worth Valley Railway and ran thus for a time, but as this locomotive has now regained the standard design presumably no great benefit was apparent on the type of work it performs on the line.

I have been associated for a very long time with the 'Power' series, which has generally concentrated on the big locomotives on the main lines, but this volume has allowed me to cover a much larger area of the network and include many scenic branch lines from which heavier motive power was banned. To me the BR Standards in general were fine, powerful and functional-looking machines — one could scarcely describe them as elegant, compared with many designs of the prewar years — but they performed very well under the far-from-ideal operating conditions that prevailed in the 1950s and '60s.

Once again my grateful thanks go to the many photographers whose work appears in the album and to the authors of the publications listed in the Bibliography, from which most of the caption details have been obtained.

Gavin Morrison
Mirfield
February 2006

Bibliography

Detailed History of British Railways Standard Steam Locomotives, Volume 2 (RCTS, 2003)
The Book of the BR Standards by Richard Derry (Irwell Press, 1997)
Locomotives Illustrated No 26 (Ian Allan, 1981)

Class 4MT

On the Southern Region

Right:
The first BR region to be allocated Class 4MT 2-6-0s in quantity was the Southern, which between December 1952 and August 1956 received 37 new examples. Of these, 10 (Nos 76053-62) went to Redhill, the remainder (Nos 76005-19/25-9/63-9) to Eastleigh. Only four months old, No 76009 simmers outside its home shed while awaiting its next duty on 30 June 1953. Subsequently transferred to Redhill, it would also be allocated to Yeovil Town, Salisbury and Bournemouth, being withdrawn from the last-named in July 1967. *B. K. B. Green*

Below:
An atmospheric picture of Eastleigh-allocated No 76006 standing at Brighton station's Platform 2 as Drummond 'M7' tank No 30108 sets off with the 5.5pm train to Horsham on 13 April 1954. *A. G. Dixon*

Above:
Seen by the offices and coaling stage, No 76016 awaits attention at its home shed of Eastleigh on 2 August 1955. It would end its working days at Guildford, in October 1966. *J. Robertson*

Below:
Eastleigh-allocated No 76014 prepares to leave Bournemouth Central with a local train for Southampton on 18 June 1957. It would ultimately be withdrawn from Bournemouth, in September 1966. *P. J. Sharpe*

Above right:
No 76014 again, this time drifting past Radipole Halt — just outside Weymouth, at the foot of the 1-in-74/50 climb from Bincombe Tunnel — with a local train from Bournemouth to Weymouth in September 1957. *T. G. Hepburn / Rail Archive Stephenson*

Right:
The only significant variation within the class was the fitting of Type 1B tenders to Nos 76053-69, which gave an additional 1,225gal water capacity over the Type 2 and 2A tenders fitted to the rest of the class. The extra capacity (giving a total of 4,725 gallons) was needed as the Southern Region had no water troughs. Coal capacity was 7 tons. This fine portrait of No 76068 on shed at Salisbury, recorded on 16 June 1957, shows the difference compared with No 76026 behind. One of four SR locomotives (the others being Nos 76063-5) only ever allocated to one shed (Eastleigh), No 76068 would be withdrawn in October 1965. *J. F. Davies / Rail Archive Stephenson*

Left:
In April and May 1955 10 members of the class, all with Type 1B tenders, were allocated new to Redhill shed. A few months after its arrival, No 76055 is seen in the company of handsome ex-SECR Class D 4-4-0s Nos 31075 and 31586 on 6 August 1955. Three other '4MTs' — Nos 76053/8/9 — were also present. *Gavin Morrison*

Centre left:
No 76059 awaits its next duty in the shed yard at Reading on 6 August 1955. *Gavin Morrison*

Bottom left:
Ready for its next duty, probably to Redhill, No 76055 stands on shed at Reading. The class was reallocated away from Redhill between May 1959 and April 1960. *Brian Morrison*

Above right:
One month before transfer from Eastleigh to Yeovil Town a well-cleaned No 76011 prepares to leave Reading General with the 11.55am to Portsmouth. The locomotive was to stay at Yeovil for just three months, moving on to Bournemouth, from where it would be withdrawn in July 1967. *M. Mensing*

Right:
No 76025, allocated to Eastleigh shed, enters North Camp station with the 1.50pm from Reading South to Redhill and London Victoria; it would be interesting to know why the British Transport Policeman was at the end of the platform. No 76025 would be transferred only once, to Bournemouth, where it would end its career in October 1965. *M. Mensing*

Above:
No 76069, seen here at Portsmouth Harbour with an up special on 24 August 1963, was the last Class 4 2-6-0 to be delivered new to the Southern Region. Having started life at Eastleigh, it would eventually be withdrawn from Guildford in June 1967. *N. Stead collection*

Left:
The Southern allocation remained basically unchanged save for the addition of Nos 76030-4, which were transferred from the Eastern Region to Brighton in November 1962, having entered service in November/December 1953 at Stratford shed in London. These locomotives differed from the rest of the class in being fitted with tablet-catchers. Still with a recess in the cabside, No 76032 heads a Redhill–Reading train along the foot of the North Downs west of Dorking Town on 3 May 1964. The locomotive would be withdrawn from Guildford shed in August 1964. *D. M. C. Hepburne-Scott / Rail Archive Stephenson*

Right:
An interloper on the Southern Region, No 76044 began its career in August 1954 at Neasden, where it stayed for almost 12 years before moving to Woodford Halse, where it was allocated when this picture was taken on 15 May 1964, so it would be interesting to know how it came to find itself at the head of the 3.54pm from Waterloo to Basingstoke, seen passing Clapham Junction. Subsequently transferred to Stoke, the locomotive would end its career at Chester, in October 1966. *Brian Stephenson / Rail Archive Stephenson*

Below:
Ex works from Eastleigh, No 76064 makes a splendid sight on shed at Salisbury in the company of a Bulleid Pacific and a Maunsell 'King Arthur' 4-6-0 on 1 October 1961. Having spent its entire career working from Eastleigh shed, the '4MT' would be withdrawn in July 1967.
Gavin Morrison

Above:
Eastleigh-based No 76063 enters Winchester Chesil — on the old Didcot, Newbury & Southampton line — with a southbound freight on 18 July 1962. The station had lost its passenger service on 7 March 1960 but was to remain open for goods until 4 April 1966. No 76063 would continue in service until April 1967. *Brian Stephenson / Rail Archive Stephenson*

Left:
No 76007 at the station end of Eastleigh shed, awaiting its next duty, on 7 September 1966. New to Eastleigh in January 1953 the locomotive was by now allocated to Bournemouth, where it would survive until July 1967. *J. Scrace*

Right:
Another of the five members of the class originally allocated to the Eastern Region at Stratford (and still with tablet-catcher recess), No 76030 stands on the scrap road at Eastleigh shed, having recently been withdrawn, on 19 April 1965. *Gavin Morrison*

Left:
Seen just days before withdrawal, No 76063 still looks to have been in reasonable condition when photographed on 14 April 1967 at the south end of Eastleigh shed, where it had been allocated throughout its career. *J. Scrace*

Right:
No 76053 well coaled up at its then home shed of Eastleigh, ready for its next duty on 22 April 1962. *Gavin Morrison*

Above:
No 76013 spent nearly all of its 11 years allocated to Eastleigh before moving to Bournemouth. Here we see it on the turntable at Eastleigh, with part of the works in the background, on 27 August 1963. Withdrawal would come in September 1966. *J. Scrace*

Below:
Summer Saturday express work for No 76013 as it passes through Eastleigh non-stop and starts the long (eight-mile) climb to Litchfield Tunnel with an express for Waterloo on 4 August 1962. *Gavin Morrison*

Above:
On a hot summer's day — 13 July 1964 — No 76060 heads across Brockenhurst Common with a down freight. New to Redhill shed, the locomotive was by now allocated to Eastleigh, where it was to spend its last 5½ years before withdrawal in December 1965. *K. L. Cook / Rail Archive Stephenson*

Below:
A couple of coaches in the new blue and grey livery are included in this up local train on 30 March 1967, headed by No 76066 and seen near Beaulieu Road. The locomotive was to remain in service at Eastleigh for a further four months, being withdrawn in July 1967. *D. M. C. Hepburne-Scott / Rail Archive Stephenson*

Left:
Transferred from the Eastern Region in 1962, No 76033 (with cabside recess) leaves Hinton Admiral station in the New Forest with a down local for Bournemouth on 23 July 1966, at which time the locomotive was allocated to Guildford. It would be withdrawn in January 1967.
Gavin Morrison

Below:
No exhaust from No 76014 on a hot July day as it pulls away from Hinton Admiral whilst working a Southampton–Bournemouth local. No 76014 spent its last two years allocated to Bournemouth, from where it was withdrawn two months after this picture was taken on 23 July 1966. *Gavin Morrison*

Above:
One of Bournemouth's allocation towards the end of Southern steam, No 76009 (minus smokebox numberplate) leaves the west end of Bournemouth Central station with a down local train on 22 July 1966. This locomotive would put in another year of service, not being withdrawn until July 1967. *Gavin Morrison*

Right:
Before the bushes on the embankments grew out of control the section of line through the woods between Bournemouth Central and Branksome used to be very pleasant for photography. No 76025, a Bournemouth locomotive, heads west towards Gas Works Junction with a train for Weymouth on 1 September 1965. *Gavin Morrison*

Left:
Not looking in the best of condition and minus its front numberplate, No 76014 of Bournemouth shed heads a six-coach train towards Gas Works Junction and Poole on 31 August 1965. The locomotive would nevertheless put in another year's service, surviving until September 1966. *Gavin Morrison*

Below:
Another very dirty Bournemouth-allocated '4MT', No 76015, pauses at Branksome station with an up local for Bournemouth Central after climbing the 1-in-50/60 up Parkstone Bank. The locomotive would be withdrawn two months after the picture was taken, on 31 August 1965. *Gavin Morrison*

Right:
Not a wisp of exhaust from the chimney of No 76007 as it heads towards Bournemouth Central near Gas Works Junction with a train from Weymouth on 1 August 1962. The distant signal in the background is 'off' for a train heading for Bournemouth West. No 76007 put in its last nine years of service at Bournemouth, being withdrawn in July 1967. *Gavin Morrison*

Below:
A fine scene at the end of Bournemouth West platform, featuring an un-rebuilt 'West Country', No 34106 *Lydford*, ready to depart with the 11.5am to Waterloo as No 76025 of Eastleigh shed arrives with a train from Salisbury. The '4MT' would end its career at Bournemouth in October 1965. *D. M. C. Hepburne-Scott / Rail Archive Stephenson*

Left:
The gasometer stands out on the skyline near Gas Works Junction, Branksome, as Bournemouth-allocated No 76014 heads for Bournemouth Central with a local train from the Somerset & Dorset line on 1 September 1965. The locomotive would have another year of service after this picture was taken.
Gavin Morrison

Below:
Pictured at Holes Bay Junction, having just joined the ex-London & South Western main line from Weymouth with the 7.35am Nottingham–Bournemouth West, Bournemouth-allocated No 76056 will have needed plenty of help on the steep gradients over the Somerset & Dorset line from Bath with its 10-coach train and would probably receive banking assistance up the 1-in-50/60 Parkstone Bank on the last leg of its journey to Bournemouth. No 76056 would be withdrawn in October 1965. *R. A. Panting*

Above:
Headed by No 76068 of Eastleigh shed, a local freight approaches Branksome station and joins the lines from Bournemouth West on 31 August 1965; the traffic will be for Poole and stations to Weymouth. No 76068 would be withdrawn less than two months later, in October 1965. *Gavin Morrison*

Below:
A photograph of No 76062, which looks to have been taken at Weymouth shed — probably in the late 1950s, as the locomotive still has the old lion-and-wheel emblem on its tender. Originally allocated to Redhill, No 76062 was to survive until October 1965. *L. King*

Left:
The first of two pictures featuring the 'South Western Suburban Rail Tour', the 100th tour organised by the Locomotive Club of Great Britain (LCGB) since 1953 — quite an achievement. Add to this the similar number of tours organised by the Railway Correspondence & Travel Society and the Stephenson Locomotive Society and others, and you can appreciate that the railway enthusiasts of the day were having a great time. No 76033, still with cabside recess for tablet-catcher, is seen passing Wokingham on its way from Staines Central to Reading General on 5 February 1967. *Brian Stephenson / Rail Archive Stephenson*

Below:
Another view of the tour, here leaving the Reading Central goods branch (at a point once known as Coley Branch Junction) *en route* for Virginia Water behind No 76058. *Brian Stephenson / Rail Archive Stephenson*

Above:
Another of the many steam specials to run on the Southern Region in 1967 was the LCGB 'Dorset Coast Express' from Waterloo, on 7 May. Having reached Wareham, the train made two return trips along the Swanage branch, the first using un-rebuilt 'West Country' No 34023 *Blackmore Vale* at one end and Standard '4MT' 2-6-0 76026 — seen here just about to leave Swanage for Wareham — at the other. Readers who have visited the delightful Swanage Railway in recent years will no doubt be able to spot the changes that have taken place since the photograph was taken. *Gavin Morrison*

Right:
From Swanage the 'Dorset Coast Express' continued to Weymouth. Ready to leave with the return working, No 76026 prepares to pilot the special up the steep climb to Bincombe Tunnels. The train engine was green-liveried Standard Class 5MT 4-6-0 No 73029, which put in a lively performance on the return to Waterloo. Both locomotives would survive until the end of Southern steam, in July 1967. *Gavin Morrison*

Above:
By the middle of 1967 Nine Elms shed was in a terrible state. No 76026, a visitor from Bournemouth, would not be withdrawn until the very end of Southern steam in July of that year but probably did little work after this picture was taken on 18 June. *I. G. Holt*

Below:
No 76064 had probably been cleaned by enthusiasts for the final days of steam on the Southern Region. Allocated to Eastleigh throughout its career, it is seen out of steam at Nine Elms shed on 3 July 1967, less than a week before withdrawal. *J. Scrace*

On the Somerset & Dorset

Above:
Transferred to Bournemouth two months earlier, No 76005 is seen working a local train near Corfe Mullen Halt, 10 miles from Bournemouth West. Photographed on 30 December 1965, it would continue in service until July 1967.
Gavin Morrison

Right:
The class became regular performers on Somerset & Dorset local services, especially south of Templecombe, although from photographic records it appears they were seldom used as pilots over the steep gradients at the northern end of the line. Here No 76011 of Bournemouth shed arrives at Henstridge with the 12.30 to Bournemouth on 5 March 1966, the last day of services on the line. The locomotive would remain in service until July 1967. *Gavin Morrison*

Left:
Midford was at the southern end of the single-line section from Bath Junction. No 76026 has just joined the double track as it pulls away with local train for Bournemouth in 1964. *M. Mensing*

Above:
Evercreech Junction, 26 miles south of Bath, was where the line to Burnham-on-Sea branched off. It was also the point at which heavy northbound trains took on a pilot for the eight-mile climb, mainly at 1 in 50, to Masbury Summit. The pilot locomotives used to wait in the centre road, shown in this picture. No 76010 will not be in need of a pilot as it prepares to leave for Bath with a stopping train on 26 September 1959. An Eastleigh engine at the time, it would be withdrawn from Bournemouth, in September 1966. *Hugh Ballantyne*

Above:
On 30 July 1955 the southbound 'Pines Express' approaches Masbury Summit behind the unusual combination of Class 2P 4-4-0 No 40634 and Eastleigh-allocated '4MT' 2-6-0 No 76012; possibly the intended train engine had failed at Bath. The Mogul would be withdrawn from Guildford, in June 1966. *Hugh Ballantyne*

Below:
A very fine picture of Eastleigh's No 76013 having just crossed Prestleigh Viaduct and at the start of the 3½-mile climb, mainly at l in 50, to Masbury Summit; there was also another climb at 1 in 50 of almost three miles before Shepton Mallet. Pictured on 26 April 1965, No 76013 would continue in service from Bournemouth until withdrawn in September 1966. *D. M. C. Hepburne-Scott / Rail Archive Stephenson*

Right:
A busy scene at Radstock as No 76027 departs with a local train for Bath on 3 April 1965. Note on the left of the picture the sub-shed (of Bath), where an LMS Sentinel was once based. No 76027 would be withdrawn from Bournemouth shed in October 1965. *Hugh Ballantyne*

Lower right:
On the last day of services on the Somerset & Dorset No 76011 of Bournemouth makes its final journey over the line with the 12.30 from Bath Green Park to Bournemouth West. The train is seen leaving Henstridge, 38 miles from Bath and with 32 still to go to Bournemouth. No 76011 would remain in service until July 1967. *Gavin Morrison*

Above:
No 76013 drifts down the l-in-50 grade out of Devonshire Hill Tunnel, on the outskirts of Bath, with a local from Bournemouth, where the locomotive was based in the mid-1960s. The tunnel was only about half a mile long, but its narrow bore made it very unpleasant for the crews, especially if a train was double-headed. Coombe Down Tunnel, on the other side of the bank, was also single-bore (and longer) but was mainly on a l-in-100 grade. No 76013 would continue working from Bournemouth until withdrawn in September 1966. *M. Mensing*

Above:
No 76056 emerges from the short twin-bore tunnel at Chilcompton, about halfway up the 7½-mile climb, at a gradient of between l in 50 and l in 70, from Radstock to Masbury Summit. The author was once warned about the presence of adder snakes in this area and later the same day discovered that this had been accurate advice. This picture was taken in 1965, in which year the locomotive would be withdrawn. *M. Mensing*

On the Scottish Region

Above:

The Scottish Region was actually the first to receive Standard '4MT' Moguls, Horwich-built Nos 76000-4 arriving at Motherwell in December 1952. Nos 76000/2/3 spent their entire careers at Motherwell, whilst 76004 strayed only as far as Greenock and Polmadie. By contrast No 76001 moved around, to Perth and, in its latter days, the 67 shed area, but its most interesting allocation was to Fort William, where it was employed mainly on Mallaig services. The only member of the class to be allocated to the West Highland line, it stayed for just over two years, from June 1960 until August 1962. During this time the author enjoyed a footplate trip on the locomotive between Fort William and Mallaig and discovered it performed very well, never being short of steam (despite being driven fairly hard, with two vans and six coaches) and gaining time against the schedule. It is seen here at the west end of Glenfinnan station, ready for the climb to the head of the glen, on 13 August 1960. *Gavin Morrison*

Right:
Having arrived at Mallaig from Fort William on 13 August 1960 Driver Adamson takes a break from the controls as his fireman prepares to take the locomotive to Mallaig shed for turning and servicing before the return journey. Note the sprig of heather in Driver Adamson's cap.
Gavin Morrison

Below:
No 76001 on the turntable at Mallaig, ready to move off for servicing, on 13 August 1960. Inside the single-road shed in the background was Gresley 'K2' No 61784, which sadly was not in steam. *Gavin Morrison*

Above:
On 12 August 1960 — the day before the author's footplate ride — No 76001 was employed on the same diagram, namely the 3.15pm Fort William. The fireman has the tablet ready to exchange it at Lochailort station as Driver Adamson slows the train for the stop. Lochailort is no longer a passing-loop on the line. *D. M. C. Hepburne-Scott / Rail Archive Stephenson*

Left:
Trains passing at Glenfinnan on 14 July 1961. Having just climbed the gradient at 1 in 50 from the viaduct, Class K1 No 62012 enters the station with the 3.15pm Fort William–Mallaig as Standard '4MT' No 76001 prepares to leave with the 2.45pm from Mallaig; the remainder of the journey will be easy work for the fireman, being downhill or on the level virtually all the way to Fort William. No 76001 would eventually be withdrawn from Ayr shed in August 1966. *E. Sucksmith*

Right:
On a dismal 10 August 1960
No 76001 storms out of Fort William
with the 3.15pm to Mallaig. On the
right is Fort William steam shed, with
a rake of coal wagons and lines
leading to the turntable and shed
yard. *Gavin Morrison*

Below:
With the wind blowing in from the
west, the exhaust puts the van and
first coach in shadow as No 76001
gets into its stride about a couple of
miles out of Mallaig on the climb to
the first summit, about a mile and a
half west of the first station, at Morar,
on 13 August 1960. This locomotive
had a red background to its front
numberplate, which was not
uncommon for Motherwell
locomotives; blue was also used,
especially by Polmadie shed.
*D. M. C. Hepburne-Scott /
Rail Archive Stephenson*

Above:
The first of the class, Motherwell's No 76000, receives attention at Carlisle Kingmoor in 1959. The locomotive would remain allocated to Motherwell until withdrawn in May 1967. *P. J. Robinson*

Below:
No 76003 recorded on 12 April 1959 at its home shed of Motherwell, where it would be allocated for its entire career until withdrawn in March 1966. *Gavin Morrison*

Right:
As mentioned previously, No 76001 was the only member of the class to be allocated to Fort William, between June 1960 and August 1962. It was normally used on the Mallaig line, but here we have a series of pictures of it working on the Oban line. The first of these shows it at Oban Junction in 1960 at the head of a light coal train, which was no doubt heading for the shed yard. *M. Mensing*

Right:
From Oban there is a very steep (1-in-50) climb for around three miles to the summit at Glencruitten, 301ft above sea level. Here No 76001 assists St Rollox-allocated Stanier Class 5 4-6-0 No 45153 away from Oban with the up Glasgow Buchanan Street express in 1960. *M. Mensing*

Left:
Having left Oban, Nos 76001 and 45153 do battle with the aforementioned climb to Glencruitten Summit. Transferred away from Fort William to Ayr in August 1962, No 76001 would remain in the 67 area until withdrawn from Ayr in August 1966. *M. Mensing*

Above:
In 1956 Scotland received a second batch of '76xxx' 2-6-0s, these being Nos 76070-4. Sent new to Motherwell from Horwich Works in October 1956, No 76071 spent its working days around Glasgow, being seen here on shed at Polmadie in August 1962. Note the large cabside numerals, which would have been applied during a visit to one of the Scottish works. *D. J. Dippie*

Below left:
No 76070 went new to Motherwell in September 1956 and except for eight months in 1964 stayed in the 66 shed area until withdrawn from Polmadie in August 1966. Here it is at the head of a returning excursion from Ayr to Motherwell not far north of Ayr. *W. Hamilton*

Above right:
No 76070 pulls out of the yard at Beattock with a down ballast train.; unfortunately there is no date for this picture. There appears to be no activity at the steam shed in the background, although this would remain open until 1967.
T. G. Hepburn / Rail Archive Stephenson

Right:
No 76000 climbing Beattock Bank between Harthope and the summit in wintry conditions on 25 February 1967, by which time the locomotive only had another three months of service. The light load would have presented no problem. *P. Brock*

Left:
No 76090 had only just arrived new from Horwich Works when this picture was taken on shed at Corkerhill on 11 June 1957; on the right of the picture is ex-LMS 'Crab' 2-6-0 No 42758 of Saltley, Birmingham, which was a long way from home. The first of a batch of 10 '4MTs' (Nos 76090-9) received by Corkerhill between June and November 1957, No 76090 was to put in 9½ years of service before being withdrawn from Beattock in December 1966. *Gavin Morrison*

Below left:
No 76091 had obviously not been cleaned for some time when photographed on 11 September 1959 heading around the south side of the triangle at Ardrossan, at the centre of which stood the shed. Save for 10 months at Parkhead in 1961 No 76091 was to spend its entire career allocated to either Corkerhill or Hurlford, being withdrawn from the latter in December 1966. *Gavin Morrison*

Top right:
No 76092 of Corkerhill shed rolls into Paisley Central with the 2.11pm to Glasgow St Enoch on 16 April 1960. This locomotive would remain allocated within the 67 area throughout its career, being retired from Hurlford in August 1966. The line west of Paisley was to close on 3 January 1983, the remaining rump being served by DMUs to/from Glasgow Central. *J. Brown*

Centre right:
On 13 June 1959, during its time allocated to Corkerhill shed (67A), No 76092 is seen passing Dalry Junction with a mineral train from Kilmarnock. Always allocated to the 67 area, the locomotive would end its career at Hurlford, in August 1966. *E. M. Patterson*

Right:
No 76099 spent its days in Scotland allocated to the 67 area and when photographed passing Kilwinning with a (very) light freight was based at Corkerhill shed. Withdrawn from Ardrossan in April 1964, it would be reinstated in September of that year and sent to Saltley, Birmingham, remaining at work on the London Midland Region until withdrawal from Colwick, near Nottingham, in August 1966. *P. J. Thorpe*

Above:
No 76095, one of the batch of 10 sent new to Corkerhill shed between June and November 1957, is seen near Elderslie, on the outskirts of Glasgow, at the head of the 4.5pm from Kilmacolm to Glasgow St Enoch. Like No 76099 it would be withdrawn in 1964 (in this case July), reinstated in September and sent to Saltley Birmingham, but was to end its working days at Chester Midland, in March 1967. *I. S. Pearsall*

Left:
Two days after a blizzard, No 76096 pulls away from Maybole station, at the head of a local service from Girvan to Glasgow on 5 March 1965. The locomotive was allocated to Ayr (67C), from which shed it would be withdrawn in December 1966. *D. Cross*

Left:
Annbank Junction, on the outskirts of Ayr, was an important junction for mineral traffic from the Ayrshire Coalfield. Here Ayr-allocated No 76097 heads a coal train from Littlemill (via Belston Junction) to Ayr Harbour on 24 May 1962. New to Corkerhill in September 1957, this locomotive was to have a working life of less than seven years, being withdrawn from Ayr as early as July 1964. *G. H. Robin*

Left:
No 76099 of Corkerhill heads a Gourock (Princes Street)–Glasgow St Enoch train across Cartsburn Viaduct on 8 November 1958. This locomotive was the last of the batch of 10 new to Corkerhill in the latter half of 1957; as already mentioned, it would be reinstated after withdrawal in July 1964, surviving thereafter on the London Midland Region until August 1966. *G. H. Robin*

Right:
Having travelled via the Kilmacolm line, an Orangemen's special consisting of 10 non-corridor coaches passes Upper Port Glasgow on 6 July 1963 behind Standard '4MT' 2-6-0 No 76092 and '4MT' 2-6-4T No 80048. *D. Cross*

Above:

In July 1957 Kittybrewster shed (61A) at Aberdeen received a batch of five new '4MT' 2-6-0s (Nos 76104-8), which together with around 14 Standard 2-6-4Ts took over most of the duties on the ex-Great North of Scotland lines, replacing various elderly 4-4-0s. When only two months old No 76105 leaves Craigellachie with the 9am from Elgin to Aberdeen in September 1957. The class put in around four years' work on the ex-GNSR before themselves being replaced by North British Type 2 diesels, amongst others. Transferred to Ferryhill shed (61B) in June 1961, No 76105 would survive until January 1966. *W. J. V. Anderson / Rail Archive Stephenson*

Below left:

Pictured in May 1958 on an unidentified passenger working on the GNSR section, No 76106 was to see just eight years of service, being withdrawn in September 1965. *T. G. Hepburn / Rail Archive Stephenson*

Above right:

A fine picture of almost new No 76108 heading a goods from Aberdeen at Keith in September 1957. Allocated initially to Kittybrewster, the locomotive was to end its career at Hurlford shed, after only nine years' service, in July 1966. *W. J. V. Anderson / Rail Archive Stephenson*

Right:

On Thursday 11 June 1959 Kittybrewster's No 76104 was engaged on a ballast train between Gartley and Huntley, about 37 miles west of Aberdeen. Along with the other '4MT' 2-6-0s this locomotive would be transferred away c1961 but would remain in service on the Scottish Region until May 1967. *Gavin Morrison*

Right:
The first of three pictures showing '4MT' 2-6-0s on coal trains. Having just joined the ex-Glasgow & South Western main line from the Muirkirk branch, Hurlford-allocated No 76092 passes Auchinleck station with a northbound coal train on 27 September 1965. The locomotive would last another 11 months, until August 1966. *C. J. Loftus*

Left:
No 76103 looks to be working hard with this coal train, seen at Cumbernauld on 26 August 1965. New to Parkhead shed (65C), Glasgow, in June 1957, the locomotive was by now based at Grangemouth. In all it would be reallocated 10 times during its brief (nine-year) career, ultimately being withdrawn from Ayr shed in June 1966. *D. M. C. Hepburne-Scott / Rail Archive Stephenson*

Left:
An excellent view of Millerhill yard in 1963, this being the scene looking south from bridge No 8, with the sorting siding on the right. Passing with a coal train on the down main line is No 76105, then allocated to Dalry Road, Edinburgh (64C) but destined to be withdrawn from Polmadie shed (66A), in January 1966. *P. Ransome-Wallis*

Right:
A superb picture of the 1.50pm Thornton–Dunfermline local stopper getting away from Cardenden in April 1959 behind No 76109. Allocated to Thornton Junction, the locomotive had been new to that shed in August 1957 and would be reallocated only once — to Dunfermline, in January 1960 — during its short career, which was to end in September 1966. *W. J. V. Anderson / Rail Archive Stephenson*

Right:
Thornton Junction's No 76111 heads a down van train past Saughton Junction (on the outskirts of Edinburgh, about a mile west of Haymarket shed), where the Aberdeen route leaves that to Glasgow and heads north towards the Forth Bridge. No 76111 was another locomotive which would manage a service life of only seven years, spent mainly at Fife sheds but ending at Bathgate, in January 1966. *G. M. Staddon / N. Stead collection*

Left:
No 76111 went new to Thornton Junction shed (62A) in July 1957, moving to Dunfermline in April 1960 and returning in February 1962. It is seen here at Dysart, south of Thornton on the old North British main line. The date is uncertain, but it seems reasonable to assume that the photograph was taken before November 1964; from that month the locomotive would be allocated to Bathgate, remaining thus until withdrawn in January 1966. *G. M. Staddon / N. Stead collection*

Left:
Of the 35 Class 4MT 2-6-0s allocated new to the Scottish Region only three were used primarily on the Dumfries–Stranraer line, or the 'Port Road', as it was commonly known. Nos 76072/3 arrived at Dumfries in October 1956, No 76112 following in September 1957; however, the last stayed for only three months before moving (in December) to Stranraer, where it would remain until withdrawn. It is pictured at Stranraer on 2 July 1961 alongside Corkerhill-based Standard 5MT No 73100, with Dumfries-allocated 'Crab' 2-6-0 No 42919 on the right; it being a Sunday morning, no locomotives were in steam.
Gavin Morrison

Above:
On the 'Port Road' the '4MTs' were responsible for both passenger and freight trains, No 76072 being seen here in charge of the 6pm Dumfries–Kirkcudbright Town on 9 July 1963. The train is entering Tarff station, which would close to passengers on 3 May 1965. The Kirkcudbright branch left the main line at Castle Douglas and was originally part of the Glasgow & South Western Railway, whereas the main line west of Newton Stewart was originally the Portpatrick & Wigtownshire Joint. *M. Mensing*

Above:
Seen just east of Newton Stewart, No 76073 approaches the town with a freight from Dumfries on 9 September 1963. Whereas No 76072 spent its entire career at Dumfries, No 76073 would move to Ayr for its final two months of service in 1966.
M. Mensing

Left:
An up freight from Kirkcudbright approaches Castle Douglas on 16 July 1963 behind No 76073. Notice the large numerals on the cabside, which would have been applied at one of the Scottish works. *M. Mensing*

Left:
No 76073 on passenger work, arriving at Kirkcudbright with the 3.30pm from Castle Douglas on 25 July 1963. Note the 67E shedplate denoting allocation to Dumfries, which shed had been recoded from 68B in July 1962. *M. Mensing*

Below left:
The 8am Kirkcudbright–Dumfries, probably considered by the locals as the morning commuter train, approaches Tarff on its journey east on 16 July 1963. *M. Mensing*

Upper right:
About 14 miles west of Dumfries is Dalbeattie, where No 76073 was photographed crossing the Ayr Viaduct with the 2.50pm from Dumfries to Kirkcudbright on 13 July 1963. This locomotive certainly seems to have followed the photographer around during his visit to the area, so presumably Nos 76072 and 76112 were under repair. *M. Mensing*

Right:
No 76073 enters Newton Stewart with a freight for Dumfries on 9 July 1963. Having already travelled some 23 miles from Stranraer the train has another 50 miles to go, which will involve some stiff gradients, especially the seven miles at l in 80 from Palnure to Gatehouse of Fleet. *M. Mensing*

Below:
On the same freight as that shown above 76073 crosses Gatehouse of Fleet Viaduct. Gatehouse of Fleet station was 4 miles from the community which it served, so clearly the photographer had his own transport to get to this remote location. The viaduct still stands today. *M. Mensing*

Above:

When new 15 Class 4MTs (Nos 76030-44) went to the Eastern Region, and 13 (76020-4/45-52) to the North Eastern. First of the class to be allocated to the North Eastern Region was No 76020 which arrived at Darlington from Doncaster Works in December 1952 and is seen passing Geneva Road, Darlington, as it leaves with an evening train to Saltburn on 31 July 1954. Note the articulated coaches behind the locomotive. *W. Rogerson / Rail Archive Stephenson*

Left:

Another picture of No 76020, this time pulling away from its home town with an evening train for Saltburn on 28 August 1954. Of the NER's first batch of five each was sent to a different shed — Darlington, York, Hull, Sunderland and Gateshead (presumably to test them around the region, although it can hardly have allowed the crews to become familiar with the type). In July 1956 No 76020 would move to Kirkby Stephen to work the Stainmore route and in April 1958 would be transferred along with that shed to the London Midland Region, on which it was to remain until withdrawn from Chester in April 1966. *R. Wilson / N. Stead collection*

Above:
Having travelled via the coast with a train of non-corridor stock from Hartlepool, No 76023 simmers in the sidings at Scarborough, its 51C (West Hartlepool) shedplate dating the photograph to between July 1955 and July 1956. The locomotive was to end its career on the London Midland Region, being withdrawn from Stoke in October 1955. *K. Hoole / N. Stead collection*

Right:
New to York shed in December 1952 as one of the NER's trial batch of five '4MTs', No 76021 later migrated to West Auckland. The locomotive is seen arriving at Durham on 20 July 1963 with a Miners' Gala special, the 7.50am from Bishop Auckland; such trains were a feature of the North East for many years. Three months later No 76021 would move to Scotland, ultimately being withdrawn from Hurlford in October 1966. *I. S. Carr*

Right:
Pictures of the class on the Eastern Region have been hard to find, but here we see No 76062 on shed at Doncaster when brand-new on 17 August 1955, before it headed south to its first allocation of Redhill. Note the Type 1B tender. The locomotive was to put in just over 10 years' service before being withdrawn from Eastleigh in October 1965. *G. Wheeler*

Above:
Several of the North Eastern locomotives were used on the famous Stainmore route between Kirkby Stephen and West Auckland. Having reversed at Kirkby Stephen East, a Penrith–Darlington train leaves the remote station at Barras, not far from Belah Viaduct, on 25 June 1956. Motive power was provided by No 76048, newly reallocated from Gateshead to Kirkby Stephen. In November 1958 this locomotive would move to the London Midland Region, in time being allocated to sheds as far apart as Skipton, Cricklewood and Croes Newydd, the last its final allocation before withdrawal in February 1967. *T. G. Hepburn / Rail Archive Stephenson*

Above right:
No 76046 heads north around the triangle at Bishop Auckland on 20 April 1957. Note the impressive gantry at the other side of the bridge. New to Gateshead but based at Bishop Auckland from June 1956, the locomotive would move to Scotland in October 1963, ending its career at Corkerhill, in October 1965. *P. B. Booth / N. Stead collection*

Right:
Displaying a 12E shedplate, No 76047 stands outside its home shed of Kirkby Stephen on 16 August 1958, the code having altered from 51H earlier that year, when the shed was transferred from the North Eastern to the London Midland Region. Inside can be seen No 76020. No 76047 was to spend four years at Kirkby Stephen before moving to Trafford Park in June 1960, ultimately being withdrawn in December 1966 from Chester Midland. *Gavin Morrison*

Above:

The Stainmore route was host to all types of BR Standard 2-6-0, and in the early 1960s Summer Saturday extras from the North East to Blackpool were nearly always hauled by '4MTs'. Photographed from the signal, No 76050 passes the summit board quoting a height of 1,370ft above sea level — about 200ft higher than Ais Gill on the Settle–Carlisle — with a train from Blackpool on 5 August 1961. The six-coach load does not seem to have caused the locomotive any difficulty on the long climb from Kirkby Stephen, and the fireman will be able to relax on the way to Barnard Castle. In October 1963 No 76050 would leave the North Eastern Region for Hawick, its final allocation ahead of withdrawal in September 1965. *Gavin Morrison*

Above right:

A view of the same train passing the signalbox, showing the track layout at the summit. *Gavin Morrison*

Right:

No 76021 passes Stainmore Summit with the summer-dated Saturdays-only Blackpool–Newcastle train on 5 August 1961. The A66 visible in the background is nowadays a very busy road, but the Stainmore route was to close in January 1962, the trackbed here now being little more than a bog. *Gavin Morrison*

Right:
The afternoon Leeds–Lancaster vans heads along the Aire Valley past the long-vanished Marley Junction, between Bingley and Keighley, on 23 May 1961. No 76051 was a North Eastern Region locomotive until transferred to Lancaster Green Ayre in April 1960, moving on to Wigan Springs Branch in February 1962 and thereafter staying on the LMR until withdrawn from Sutton Oak in April 1967. *Gavin Morrison*

Above:
In the early 1960s '4MT' 2-6-0s were allocated to Lancaster Green Ayre and were frequently seen in the Aire Valley, especially on van trains but also on some passenger workings. No 76022 passes slowly around the sharp curve of the Shipley triangle (nowadays the site of the Leeds–Skipton direct platforms) on 31 July 1961. Having been transferred from the North Eastern Region in April 1960, this locomotive would stay for 22 months before moving on to other London Midland Region sheds and ending its days at Oxley in August 1966. *Gavin Morrison*

Below:
Another picture of No 76022, taking water before moving off shed at Leeds Holbeck on 9 August 1961. Being serviced on the left is one of the shed's Caprotti Class 5s, No 44753. *Gavin Morrison*

Below right:
Pictured leaving Keighley, a Whitsuntide special from Bradford Forster Square to Morecambe provides a means of getting No 76048 back home to Skipton on 15 May 1959. The '4MT' is piloting Manningham-based ex-LMS 'Crab' 2-6-0 No 42702 on a rake of non-corridor stock. One of only two such locomotives believed allocated to Skipton, No 76048 had been transferred from the North East in November 1958 and would stay until May 1959, ultimately ending its career at Croes Newydd, in February 1967. *Gavin Morrison*

Above:
In the days when there were four tracks between Shipley and Leeds, No 76051 is again seen in charge of the afternoon Leeds–Lancaster vans, this time on 6 June 1961. Pictured just north of Apperley Bridge, the train is passing Bradford Esholt Sewage Works, which once had an internal railway system of its own. *Gavin Morrison*

Below:
Rounding Whitehall Curve, No 76022 makes a dramatic exit from Leeds City as it heads north with the afternoon train to Morecambe, made up of non-corridor stock, on 9 July 1960. The external condition of the locomotive was not untypical for Lancaster's allocation around this time. *Gavin Morrison*

Above:

No '4MT' 2-6-0s were allocated to the LMR until December 1956, when No 76075 arrived at Sutton Oak, to be followed in February 1957 by Nos 76076-9; thereafter Nos 76080-9 were shared between Lower Darwen, Lancaster and Trafford Park. This fine study depicts No 76085 ready to leave Nottingham Midland with a stopping train along the Erewash Valley to Chesterfield on 31 May 1957; at this time the locomotive was just over a month old and still allocated to Leicester Midland, which shed was to retain its two '76xxx' Class 4MTs (Nos 76085/6) for only two months before losing them to Saltley, Birmingham. In all No 76085 would be transferred seven times within the London Midland Region, ultimately being withdrawn from Annesley shed in July 1966. *J. P. Wilson / Rail Archive Stephenson*

Above:

A fine study of No 76076 at its home shed of Sutton Oak, six months after it arrived new from Horwich Works in December 1956. This locomotive was to work for one month short of 10 years, remaining at Sutton Oak until withdrawal in November 1966. *J. F. Davies / Rail Archive Stephenson*

Left:
An up part-fitted freight headed
by Saltley's No 76087 heads along the
ex-Great Western main line between
Solihull and Widney Manor on
14 September 1957. This was an
unusual locomotive for the route,
such trains normally being hauled by a
Stanier Class 5MT 4-6-0. *M. Mensing*

Below:
Saltley-allocated No 76087 waits
to leave Birmingham New Street
with the 1.45pm to Cromer Beach
and Yarmouth Beach via Leicester and
the M&GN line on 28 December
1957. New to Trafford Park shed
in Manchester, the locomotive
would be transferred a further
six times before being withdrawn
from Wolverhampton Oxley
during January 1967. *M. Mensing*

Right:
The London Midland Region's allocation of '4MT' 2-6-0s was bolstered in 1958 when the ex-Great Central line was transferred from the Eastern Region. New from Doncaster Works in May 1954, No 76037 was one a batch of 10 allocated initially to Neasden. Photographed alongside a DMU at Aylesbury shed on 26 September 1964, it displays a 14B shedplate suggesting allocation to Kentish Town, although records reveal that the locomotive was by now based at Cricklewood. It would remain on the London Midland Region for the rest of its career, which was to end at Croes Newydd in April 1967.
Brian Stephenson / Rail Archive Stephenson

Right:
Having been transferred from Neasden a year previously, No 76042 is pictured on shed at Cricklewood on 7 July 1963. The locomotive would remain on the London Midland Region until withdrawn from Oxley in June 1966. *R. A. Panting*

Left:
Originally allocated to Stratford shed in East London and fitted with a tablet-catcher, No 76032 subsequently moved to March shed, being seen ready to leave Northampton on 17 June 1961 with the 5.10pm to Peterborough East. Transferred away from March shed in November 1962, the locomotive would see out its days on the Southern Region, at Brighton and then Guildford, withdrawal coming in August 1964. *M. Mensing*

Above:
No 76043 heads south with a train of empty iron-ore wagons between Solihull and Widney Manor, on the ex-Great Western main line between Birmingham Snow Hill and Leamington, on 7 August 1964. New to Neasden but by now allocated to Saltley, the locomotive would be withdrawn from Machynlleth shed during September 1966. *M. Mensing*

Below:
Enthusiasts who have known steam only in preservation will find it hard to believe that locomotives used to run in the condition demonstrated here by No 76038, seen heading the down 'Cambrian Coast Express' about ¼ mile west of Hanwood station, which had closed to passengers on 12 September 1960. The picture was taken on 9 July 1966, by which time the locomotive was allocated to Machynlleth. Withdrawal was to follow just two months later, in September 1966. *M. Mensing*

Left:
No 76040 pauses at Aberdovey whilst working a summer-dated Saturdays-only train from Pwllheli to the Midlands on 13 August 1966. Records show the locomotive as allocated to Saltley, but in practice it had probably just been transferred to Croes Newydd (witness its lack of shedplate), from which shed it was to continue in service until April 1967. *Gavin Morrison*

Below:
The 6.50pm Aberystwyth–Shrewsbury mail train, headed by No 76040, about a mile west of Llanbrynmair station (which had closed to passengers on 14 June 1965) on 27 August 1966. *M. Mensing*

Right:
BR Standard '4MTs' double-heading. Half a mile north of Pontdolgoch station (closed 14 June 1965) 4-6-0 No 75052 pilots 2-6-0 No 76095 with the Aberystwyth portion of the down 'Cambrian Coast Express' on 27 August 1966. Withdrawn in July 1964 but reinstated, No 76095 was by now allocated to Chester Midland shed, whence it would be withdrawn for the second and final time in March 1967; No 75052 was to survive until August 1967.
M. Mensing

Class 3MT

On the Eastern and North Eastern Regions

Above:
Built at Swindon Works, the Class 3MT 2-6-0s numbered just 20 locomotives, shared between the North Eastern Region at Darlington (Nos 77000-4/10-4) and the Scottish Region. No 77012 is seen here at Scarborough Falsgrave Road on 24 July 1954 when only a month old. It carries an express headcode, so this is possibly the same working as that shown opposite. *K. Hoole / N. Stead collection*

Left:
The first of two pictures featuring No 77013, sent new to Darlington shed in July 1954. In this view, recorded early in its career, on 19 July 1955, the locomotive is passing Redcar East with a Saltburn–Darlington train. Later in the year it would be transferred away to Whitby and then further transferred within the York division, before ending up at Stourton, Leeds. *L. A. Strudwick / N. Stead collection*

Right:

Closed in stages from May 1958, the route from Saltburn to Scarborough featured gradients as steep as 1 in 39 and coastal views as fine as any to be had from a train. Here Darlington's No 77012 is hard at work on the climb to Ravenscar; despite its express headcode there will be little opportunity for high speed on its journey to Scarborough on 2 September 1954. *T. G. Hepburn / Rail Archive Stephenson*

Below:

No 77004 has just arrived at Scarborough Falsgrave Road with a train from Whitby, as 'B16' 4-6-0 No 61470 leaves, while just visible on the right is Class D49 'Hunt' 4-4-0 No 62756 *The Brocklesby*. The picture is undated but was most likely taken during the late summer of 1958, when No 77004 was allocated to Whitby; transferred no fewer than 13 times during its 12½ years of service on the North Eastern Region, this locomotive would end its career at Stourton, Leeds, in December 1966. *T. G. Hepburn / Rail Archive Stephenson*

Above:
A very fine picture of No 77012 climbing towards Goathland on what is now the North Yorkshire Moors Railway.
The rolling stock hardly gives the impression that this is an express working, as indicated by the headlamps.
The original caption on the back of the print states that the photograph was taken *c*1958; corroborating this is the 50F shedplate denoting allocation to Whitby, where the locomotive was based between November 1955 and December 1958.
C. Ord / Rail Archive Stephenson

Above:
The first of three photographs taken at Whitby Town during the summer of 1958 and featuring No 77012 shunting the empty stock for a train to Malton. Also visible in this picture are a Metro-Cammell DMU (later Class 101) and Thompson 'L1' 2-6-4T No 67754 with a train for Middlesbrough. *M. Mensing*

Right:
No 77012 draws the empty stock out of the station and towards the carriage sidings, these being located near the locomotive shed, a few hundred yards from the platform end. *M. Mensing*

Right:
The Class 101 DMU has now moved into the centre road, and No 77012 stands on its own at the platform. *M. Mensing*

Left:
During its time allocated to Hull Dairycoates (53A) No 77001 leaves Pontefract Monkhill with the 7.57am stopping train to Wakefield and Bradford during 1957. No 77001 would be transferred 10 times around the North Eastern Region, ultimately being withdrawn from Goole, in January 1966.
P. Cookson / N. Stead collection

Below:
No 77001 arrives at Bridlington with the 11.25 from Hull; the shedplate appears to be 53A (Hull Dairycoates), dating the picture to between June 1959 and January 1960. The locomotive would remain on the North Eastern Region, working from nine different sheds until withdrawn (from Goole) in January 1966.
K. Hoole / N. Stead collection

Right:
No 77001 on shed at York on 18 October 1961. At this time the locomotive was allocated to Hull Dairycoates, which shed had changed code from 53A to 50B in January 1960 when incorporated into the York area. *Gavin Morrison*

Below:
No 77000 trundles along the Hull Docks line with some mineral wagons for Albert Docks while working from Eastern Docks as pilot No 36 on 17 February 1962. New to Darlington shed, the pioneer '3MT' 2-6-0 was by now allocated to Hull Dairycoates. *D. P. Leckonby / N. Stead collection*

Above:
Allocated to Gateshead when this picture was taken on 7 July 1960, No 77011 passes Hall Dene at the head of an excursion to Redcar. The locomotive would be allocated to nine different sheds in a career lasting just under 12 years; it would also be the only member of the class to be allocated to the London Midland Region, ending its working life in February 1966 after a 15-month spell at Northwich. *G. M. Staddon / N. Stead collection*

Left:
No 77002 pilots a '76xxx' across Smardale Viaduct, between Kirkby Stephen and Tebay, with a summer-dated working from the North East to Blackpool. Close by is the other Smardale Viaduct — on the Settle–Carlisle line — where the line to Tebay passed under the ex-Midland route. Regrettably the picture is undated, the line closed in January 1962. From West Auckland No 77002 would move home another seven times, ending its career at York, in June 1967. *C. Ord / Rail Archive Stephenson*

Above:
Another train from the North East to Blackpool approaches Tebay on 5 August 1961. The leading locomotive this time is No 77003, piloting Ivatt Class 4MT 2-6-0 No 43126. *Gavin Morrison*

Right:
Another picture of No 77003, this time at Bishop Auckland in August 1961. *N. Stead collection*

Left:
It was perhaps inevitable that the Stainmore line would fall victim to the Beeching axe. The end came on 20 January 1962, when to mark the occasion the RCTS ran a special from Darlington to Tebay and return. The locomotives used were a pair of well-turned-out Standard 2-6-0s from West Auckland shed, Nos 77003 and 76049 being seen passing Bowes *en route* for Stainmore. No 77003 was to stay until transferred in February 1964 to Stourton, Leeds, whence it would be withdrawn in December 1966, whereas No 76049 would move in 1963 to the Scottish Region, ultimately being withdrawn from Bathgate in January 1966. *Gavin Morrison*

Left:
The Stainmore line crosses the famous Belah Viaduct, built in 1859 with a maximum height of 196ft and 1,047ft long. Note the remote signalbox at the far side — what a place to work in winter! It could be reached by road, but this involved opening and closing no fewer than six gates. To mark the closure of the line the RCTS ran a farewell tour using '3MT' No 77003 and '4MT' No 76049, seen heading west over the viaduct on the last day, 20 January 1962; the special had left Darlington at 10.46am but would not return until 11pm, so as to be the last train over the line, passing Stainmore Summit at 10pm. *Gavin Morrison*

Left:
The RCTS special of 20 January 1962 passes the delightful station at Ravenstondale, just six miles from Tebay. The station building survives as an attractive private dwelling, but much of the trackbed between here and Tebay now forms the basis of the A685 road. *Gavin Morrison*

Right:
With 77003 blowing off the last train on the Stainmore line approaches Tebay, where, some 58 miles 58 chains from Darlington, the line joined the West Coast route. *Gavin Morrison*

Right:
Nos 77003 and 76049 on arrival at Tebay with the last train from Kirkby Stephen, 20 January 1962. The pair will shortly move off to be serviced in the North Eastern yard.
Gavin Morrison

Below:
There was no North Eastern shed at Tebay, locomotives being serviced in the yard, where there was a large water tower. No 77003 takes water on 20 January 1962— the last time these facilities would be used.
Gavin Morrison

Left:
By the mid-1960s all 10 of the North Eastern Region's '3MT' 2-6-0s had at some stage been allocated to Stourton, Leeds, where they primarily replaced the shed's allocation of Midland 0-6-0s on local freight duties. The impressive view from the top of the signalbox steps at Wortley Junction on 17 September 1963, showing the track layout and also (in the background) the disused platforms at Holbeck Low Level (closed since 7 July 1958) and the bridge carrying the old Great Northern main line into Leeds Central. No 77001 has just arrived with coal for the gasworks, which it will leave in the siding for collection. *Gavin Morrison*

Left:
Having dropped off some wagons for the gasworks at Wortley Junction, Leeds, on 20 September 1963, No 77001 prepares to leave to carry out further shunting duties along the Midland main line towards Shipley. The locomotive had been transferred to Stourton in September 1963 but would stay for just three months before moving to Farnley Junction, thereafter spending short periods at Manningham, Hull Dairycoates and finally Goole, its last allocation before withdrawal in January 1966. *Gavin Morrison*

Right:
The Class 3MT 2-6-0s were seldom used on passenger duties around Leeds, but here we see No 77002 passing Wortley Junction on 17 September 1963 with a southbound empty-stock train. Visible in the background is Wortley North signalbox, which primarily controlled the lines to Harrogate out of Leeds Central. No 77002 was to enjoy two spells at Stourton — 14 months from September 1963 and three from July 1966 — before ending its career at York in June 1967. *Gavin Morrison*

Right

No 77000 has just arrived at Calverley & Rodley to carry out some shunting work on 19 August 1966. Stourton was to be its last allocation; having been transferred from Darlington (to which shed it had returned in 1963) in May 1964, the locomotive would be withdrawn in December 1966. *Gavin Morrison*

Right

In poor external condition for a prestige duty, No 77012 hauls an inspection saloon for BR management through the centre road at Durham *en route* for Newcastle on 14 April 1966. Having been transferred no fewer than 10 times, the locomotive was by now allocated to York, where it would end its career in June 1967. *I. S. Carr*

Left:

On 14 February 1964, by which time it was allocated to Stourton, No 77013 found itself at Toton shed, on the London Midland Region. The circumstances behind its appearance at this unlikely location are a mystery; presumably it had somehow worked its way south to the Nottingham area via the Midland main line. The locomotive was to see out its days at the Leeds shed, being withdrawn in March 1966. *N. E. Preedy*

On the Scottish Region

Above:
Of the class of 20 locomotives, 10 '3MTs' were allocated from new to the Scottish Region. The first batch of five (Nos 77005-9) shared between Hamilton and Perth, whereas the later batch (Nos 77015-9) went to Hurlford shed. New to Perth the previous month, No 77008 is seen near Dunkeld with the 1.35pm Perth–Blair Atholl stopping train on 15 May 1954. It was to remain at its first home for only seven months before moving to Motherwell, from which shed it would be withdrawn in June 1966. *W. J. V. Anderson / Rail Archive Stephenson*

Left:
Allocated to Hamilton, where it went new in March 1954, No 77005 leaves Glasgow Central on 14 June 1954 with the 3.55pm Cathcart Inner Circle train, seen crossing the River Clyde. The locomotive would never stray far from Glasgow, being withdrawn from Motherwell in June 1963.
W. J. Cameron

Above:
No 77018 at Cowlairs Works, alongside an ex-North British Class N15 tank. The date was 23 June 1957, so the '3MT' was probably awaiting its first major overhaul, after almost three years in service. This was another member of the class to spend all its time at Hurlford, until withdrawal in November 1966. *Brian Morrison*

Above:
Obviously taken on a very wet day, this photograph is interesting in that it shows No 77005 with the wider type of chimney fitted to the BR Class 4MTs. This modification was probably carried out at Cowlairs Works, which applied the name of each locomotive's home shed (in this case Motherwell) to the buffer-beam. As No 77005 has the later style of lion-and-wheel emblem on its tender the photograph was most likely taken in the early 1960s. *Ian Allan Library*

Left:
Typical of the work performed by the '3MTs' around Ayrshire during the first 10 years of their careers, a Clyde Coast local train leaves Glasgow St Enoch on 30 May 1961 behind No 77017. Allocated to Hurlford throughout its career, this locomotive would survive in service until November 1966.
D. T. Greenwood / Rail Archive Stephenson

Centre left:
No 77017 appears to be about as black as its exhaust as it leaves Ayr at the head of the 5.8pm to Kilmarnock, complete with Royal Mail van.
C. E. Weston

Bottom left:
Somewhat surprisingly loaded to six coaches, the 9.55 Muirkirk–Carstairs departs Inches station on 5 March 1961, hauled by Hurlford's No 77018. This station was to close on 5 October 1964, the locomotive surviving it by two years. *D. Cross*

Above right:
The '3MTs' were not usually seen in the east of Scotland save during a period of two years from October 1963, when No 77009 was transferred to Grangemouth. The locomotive is shown approaching Millerhill yard on 9 May 1964 with a train of empty mineral wagons. Reallocated to Motherwell in October 1965, it would be withdrawn in May 1966.
G. M. Staddon / N. Stead collection

Right:
The 1.35pm Dalmellington–Kilmarnock passes Holehouse Junction behind No 77016. The superb sweeping curve and immaculate embankments are worth noting. By the mid-1960s this type of work was fast diminishing, due to line closures and the introduction of DMUs, and this was in fact the last steam-hauled passenger train on the Dalmellington branch, on 4 April 1964. No 77016 was to be yet another lifelong Hurlford engine, surviving until March 1966. *D. Cross*

On the Southern Region

Above:
No 77014 was probably the most photographed member of the class, on account of its being the only example to be allocated to the Southern Region, in the last years of steam. Transferred to Guildford in March 1966, it lasted until steam on the Southern ended in July 1967. During this period it was used to pilot expresses diverted (due to electrification work on the South Western main line) via the Mid-Hants line and also appeared on railtours. It is seen here at Guildford on 18 June 1967. *Brian Stephenson / Rail Archive Stephenson*

Left:
On what may very well have been the only occasion that a '77xxx' hauled a Pullman train, No 77014 pilots unrebuilt Bulleid 'West Country' Pacific No 34102 *Lapford* out of Alton at the head of the down 'Bournemouth Belle' on 18 September 1966. This stretch of line nowadays forms part of the Mid-Hants Railway, known as the 'Watercress Line'. *Brian Stephenson / Rail Archive Stephenson*

Above:
Having managed to get ahead of the 'Bournemouth Belle' as it tackled the steep gradient between Alton and Medstead on the Mid-Hants line, the photographer obtained another shot of Nos 77014 and 34102 as they sped downhill past Ropley on 18 September 1966. *Brian Stephenson / Rail Archive Stephenson*

Below:
On 16 October 1966 No 77014 participated in the Locomotive Club of Great Britain's 'Dorset & Hants Rail Tour' from Waterloo. The train is passing the old Spetisbury Halt (between Blandford Forum and Broadstone), which had closed on 17 September 1956. *Brian Stephenson / Rail Archive Stephenson*

Class 2MT

Above:
The '78xxx' Class 2MT 2-6-0s were excellent branch-line engines and were almost identical to the Ivatt 2-6-0s. The class comprised 65 locomotives, of which the Western Region received the first 10. This fine portrait was recorded of No 78003 when the locomotive was new at Swindon on 1 February 1953, in lined black livery and destined to be allocated to Oswestry. The locomotive would have a working life of just under 14 years, being withdrawn in December 1966 from Shrewsbury shed. *R. A. Wheeler / Rail Archive Stephenson*

On the Western Region

Right:
Always different from the others, the Western Region painted its locomotives variously in lined and unlined green livery, mainly during their first major overhauls. This picture shows No 78000, (which had entered service in December 1952) in unlined green livery at Andover on a running-in turn after being out of traffic for 10 months at Swindon Works. There is no date, but as the later style of lion-and-wheel emblem is carried on the tender the photograph was probably taken in the late 1950s. No 78000 was to end its career on the London Midland Region, at Derby, in June 1965. *G. Wheeler*

Right:
Delivered to Oswestry shed between December 1952 and April 1953, Nos 78000-9 were the only BR Standard 2-6-0s to be allocated new to the Western Region. No 78006 arrived in March 1953 but in September was transferred to Machynlleth; here it is seen preparing to leave Llanfyllin station for Oswestry on 5 March 1956. This ex-Cambrian branch southwest of Oswestry was to close on 18 January 1965. *Hugh Ballantyne*

Below :
Another picture of No 78006, this time standing by the cliff-face at the back of its home shed on 28 March 1959, by which time it had gained lined green livery. The locomotive would remain allocated to Machynlleth until September 1962. *Gavin Morrison*

Above:
No 78002 completes a line-up of motive power on 21 June 1958 at Machynlleth, which by this time was its home shed; also on view are ex-GWR 'Dukedog' 4-4-0 No 9021 and 'Small Prairie' No 4549. Transferred along with Machynlleth to the London Midland Region in August 1963, the '2MT' would be withdrawn from Lostock Hall in June 1966. *Gavin Morrison*

Below:
Activity at Moat Lane Junction on 7 June 1960. Ivatt '2MT' No 46523 is in the bay, in the centre of the picture can be seen the rear of the 2.30pm Aberystwyth–Oswestry (headed by ex-GWR 'Manor' 4-6-0 No 7801 *Anthony Manor*), whilst on the right is BR Standard '2MT' No 78002 with the 4.20pm Newtown–Machynlleth. *Hugh Ballantyne*

Above:
Seen crossing from the Stroud line onto the Bristol main line No 78006 passes Standish Junction signalbox with a southbound freight on 20 July 1965. The locomotive was by now allocated to Gloucester Horton Road, from which shed it would be withdrawn in October 1966. *Hugh Ballantyne*

Below:
New to Oswestry shed in April 1953, No 78009 was transferred in July of that year to Worcester, where it was to remain allocated for nearly 10 years. Transferred to Gloucester in March 1963, the locomotive would be withdrawn in February 1964. No 78009 is seen at Chipping Campden on the Worcester-Paddington line. *Ian Allan Library*

Above:
Between December 1953 and March 1954 10 Class 2MT 2-6-0s were delivered new to the North Eastern Region, being allocated to West Auckland (Nos 78010-8) and Kirkby Stephen (78019) sheds, primarily for freight work over the Stainmore line; passenger services gained new '82xxx' 2-6-2Ts. Only six months old, No 78019 stands on the turntable at Darlington station on 28 August 1954. After a working life of nearly 13 years it would be withdrawn from Crewe South in November 1966 and subsequently purchased for preservation. Following 37 years' inactivity it has recently been returned to working order on the Great Central Railway. *A. R. Carpenter / N. Stead collection*

Right:
Having descended from Stainmore Summit, No 78018 arrives at Kirkby Stephen East with a train of coke empties on 31 August 1956, its 51H shedplate revealing it to be a Kirkby Stephen locomotive. It would be transferred to the London Midland Region at Chester in April 1960, thereafter moving five more times and ending its working life at Shrewsbury, in April 1966. The locomotive survives in preservation at the Darlington Railway Centre, where it is currently undergoing restoration. *J. F. Davies / Rail Archive Stephenson*

Left:
In the first of a sequence of photographs taken on 16 August 1958 No 78013, by now transferred to Kirkby Stephen, blasts its way towards Stainmore Summit. Banked by No 78017, the train is passing through the lonely Barras station, which when opened on 26 March 1861 was the highest in England. *Gavin Morrison*

Below:
Nos 78013 and 78017 at Stainmore Summit signalbox (1,370ft). Having banked the train from Kirkby Stephen East, mainly at 1 in 60, No 78017 will now act as pilot through to West Auckland. *Gavin Morrison*

Right:
Nos 78017 and 78013 leave Stainmore Summit for West Auckland. Both locomotives would later be transferred with Kirkby Stephen shed to the London Midland Region, No 78017 being withdrawn from Shrewsbury in December 1966, and No 78013 from Bolton in May 1967. *Gavin Morrison*

Right:
This being a Saturday evening, the crew were obviously in a hurry to get home, and the train descended very quickly from Stainmore to Bowes and then took the line to West Auckland, where it is seen passing Coal Road level crossing at 7.30pm. *Gavin Morrison*

Left:
Of the 10 members of the class that went new to the North East six (Nos 78010-5) were allocated for a time to Northallerton, which had a small two-road shed situated at a lower level than the East Coast main line. With the station visible on the right, No 78010 keeps company with local 'K1' 2-6-0 No 62044 on 30 March 1962. The '2MT' would be reallocated to Polmadie, Glasgow, in March 1963, thereafter wandering far and wide before withdrawal in April 1964 from Crewe South.
Gavin Morrison

Below:
Another view at Northallerton shed, this time showing No 78014 with WD 2-8-0 No 90430 on 5 March 1961. No 78014 would be reallocated to Darlington in March 1963 but withdrawn from Trafford Park, Manchester in September 1965.
Gavin Morrison

Right:
Nos 78020 and 78021 went new (in April and May 1954 respectively) to Kettering shed, where they remained for around five years. No 78021 is shown approaching Godmanchester — just east of Huntingdon, on the ex-Great Northern/Great Eastern joint line — on 13 May 1959 at the head of a Kettering–Cambridge train. Passenger services at Godmanchester finished one month later. No 78021 was to remain on the London Midland Region, ending its working life at Lostock Hall in May 1967.
D. M. C. Hepburne-Scott / Rail Archive Stephenson

On the London Midland Region

Below:
A picture taken at Huntingdon East station, showing how similar the Standard Class 2MTs were to the earlier Ivatt Class 2 2-6-0s. For 10 months in 1959 No 78028, the second locomotive, was allocated to Kettering, where No 46404 was also based. *T. G. Hepburn / N. Stead collection*

Left:
Millhouses shed at Sheffield (19B, later 41C) received Nos 78022-5 new in May/June 1954. No 78025 is shown negotiating the sharp curve at Long Eaton Junction, heading the 2.30pm local stopping train from Nottingham Midland to Chesterfield on 9 May 1955. *J. P. Wilson / Rail Archive Stephenson*

Right:
No 78025 simmers in one of the centre roads at Sheffield Midland station on 26 March 1961, when it was still allocated to Millhouses shed (19B). It would move on in January 1962, seeing service at several more sheds, including Tweedmouth (NER) and March (ER), before ending its career back on the LMR at Gorton, Manchester, in February 1965. *J. C. Hayden*

Below:
Seen just west of Edale, No 78023 heads west along the delightful Hope Valley with the 12.50pm Sheffield Midland–Chinley on 3 October 1959. After it left Millhouses in January 1962, this locomotive was transferred eight times, ending its career in May 1967 at Bolton. *M. Mensing*

Below:
Later in its career No 78022 was allocated to Lostock Hall, where it seen in December 1963 and where it would end its BR career in September 1966. Happily it survives in preservation and can now be seen on the Keighley & Worth Valley Railway. *W. D. Cooper*

Above:
One of five '2MTs' allocated to Bank Hall, Liverpool, in December 1954, No 78040 had been transferred to Wigan by the time this photograph was taken, being seen on shed at its new home on 4 June 1957. Allocated to the North West throughout its life, it would be withdrawn in January 1966 from Lostock Hall. *R. J. Buckley*

Below:
New in November 1954 to Preston, where it would stay until September 1961, No 78037 was one of the locomotives which sustained superficial damage when its home shed caught fire in June 1960. However, this cannot have been too serious, for the locomotive would be back in traffic within three months. *D. T. Greenwood / Rail Archive Stephenson*

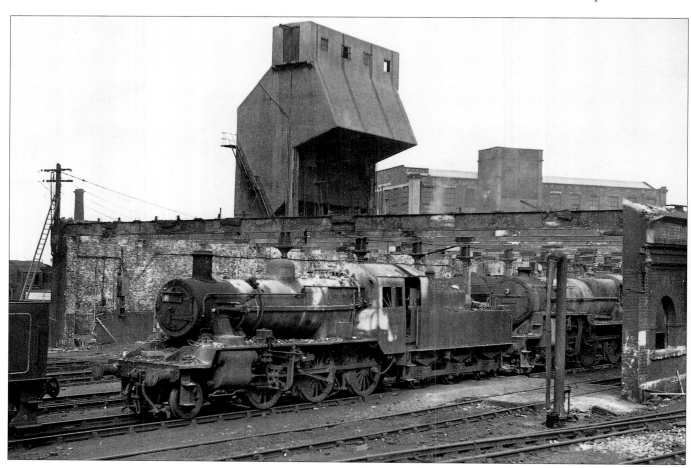

Above:
No 78037, obviously ex works following repair, on empty-stock duty at the north end of Crewe station on 27 September 1960. Its career would come to an end in May 1967 at Lostock Hall, only a few miles from where it had started.
M. Mensing

Below:
No 78063 at Newton Heath shed, Manchester, during June 1960, at which time it was still allocated to Wigan Central, where it had been based since new in November 1956. Transferred to Willesden in May 1963, the locomotive would end its career at Shrewsbury, in December 1966. *J. E. Wilkinson*

Left:
In 1962/3 Nos 78036 and 78037 both spent short periods based at Skipton. In the first month of the 'big freeze', No 78036 pulls away from Hellifield with a stopping train for Heysham on 26 January 1963. This locomotive would ultimately be withdrawn from Shrewsbury, in December 1966. *Gavin Morrison*

Centre left:
The '2MTs' were seldom seen in the Bradford area, the exception being No 78014, allocated to Manningham shed between April and December 1964 and pictured at Forster Square station on 31 August. It would be withdrawn from Trafford Park, Manchester, in September 1965. *B. G. Tweed / N. Stead collection*

Lower left:
Headed by No 78008, a one-time Cambrian engine by now reallocated to Wolverhampton Stafford Road, the 7.15pm Stourbridge Junction–Wolverhampton Low Level approaches Tipton (Five Ways) on Monday 11 June 1962. Anticipating the closure in 1963 of Stafford Road shed the locomotive would move in November 1962 to nearby Oxley, continuing in service there until October 1966. *M. Mensing*

Above right:
On 23 April 1966 a well-turned-out No 78036 of Crewe South shed was diagrammed to work from Wellington to Crewe with the 'St Georges' railtour, organised by the West Midlands branch of the Railway Correspondence & Travel Society. The train is seen passing Wollerton Halt, which had closed to passengers on 9 September 1963. *M. Mensing*

Right
Another view of the same railtour, this time at Over & Wharton, which station had closed to passengers on 16 June 1947. The train had reversed down the branch. In November 1966 No 78036 would be transferred to Shrewsbury, withdrawal following one month later. *M. Mensing*

Above:
The Scottish Region received just 10 Class 2MT 2-6-0s (Nos 78045-54), delivered October-December 1955. Allocated to Kittybrewster shed in Aberdeen, No 78045 was normally based at Fraserburgh, for working the St Coombs branch. The branch train, which certainly didn't have enough passengers to warrant three coaches, is seen entering Fraserburgh on 12 June 1959, the sub-shed being visible just beyond the locomotive. *Gavin Morrison*

Above right:
Classified as a light railway and running through sand-dunes and a golf course beside Fraserburgh Bay, the St Coombs branch was just over five miles long, with an intermediate halt at Cairnbulg. No 78045 arrives *en route* to Fraserburgh on 12 June 1959. *Gavin Morrison*

Right:
No 78045 stands at St Coombs, the end of the line, as the grass receives attention from a gentleman with a large scythe. The branch was to close on 3 May 1965, No 78045 moving thereafter to Keith shed, but like three other Scottish-allocated members of the class it would be withdrawn from Bathgate, in January 1966. *Gavin Morrison*

Left:
New in October 1955, Nos 78046 and 78047 were allocated to Hawick shed for use on local trains around the Border Country. Having just emerged from Cowlairs Works following what was probably its first major repair, No 78047 stands on shed at Eastfield on 2 September 1958, awaiting running-in before returning home. *Gavin Morrison*

Below:
After a few years Hawick shed also gained Nos 78048 and 78049, which had been new to St Margarets. Headed by No 78048, the 8.25am from St Boswells crosses the Royal Border Bridge as it approaches Berwick-upon-Tweed on 1 June 1962. Opened by Queen Victoria in August 1850, this famous structure is 2,152ft long, 126ft high and has 28 61ft 6in arches. *M. Mensing*

Above:
Another view of the Royal Border Bridge, this time with No 78049 arriving at Berwick-upon-Tweed with the 4pm from St Boswells on 23 May 1962. This locomotive had moved to Hawick from St Margarets shed in June 1959 but was to return in January 1966 ahead of withdrawal that August. *M. Mensing*

Below:
The 4pm from St Boswells, formed of five vans and a coach, stands at Berwick-upon-Tweed on 23 May 1962, having arrived behind No 78049. *M. Mensing*

Above:
Filling in its 26-minute scheduled waiting-time, No 78048 stands at Kelso station before continuing its journey to Berwick-upon-Tweed with the 4pm from St Boswells on 26 May 1962. *M. Mensing*

Above right:
No 78048 leaves St Boswells with the 4pm train to Berwick-upon-Tweed on 31 August 1962. Transferred to Hawick from St Margarets in July 1960, No 78048 would stay until withdrawn in July 1964. *T. G. Hepburn / Rail Archive Stephenson*

Right:
No 78046 waits to leave Kelso with the single-coach 2.21pm to St Boswells on 2 September 1963. The '2MTs' would remain the regular motive power for local trains in the Borders until services ceased in 1964. *T. G. Hepburn / Rail Archive Stephenson*

Left:
The fireman on the 2.21pm Berwick-upon-Tweed–St Boswells on 30 May 1962 must have had an easy shift, the train — pictured just after leaving Kelso — comprising just one coach! A Hawick locomotive for 10 years, No 78047 would eventually be withdrawn from St Margarets shed, in September 1966. *M. Mensing*

Left:

In December 1956 No 78052 was transferred to Inverness, probably to replace '16xx' pannier tanks on the Dornoch branch, which was as far north as the '2MTs' worked. Hauling coach SC6603M, two box wagons and an LNER brake van, it is shown approaching The Mound from Dornoch on 1 May 1957. Reallocated to St Margarets for two months from September 1958, this locomotive would then move back south, to Aviemore, staying for almost four years before ending its career at Bathgate in January 1966.
Hugh Ballantyne

Below left:

A superb picture of No 78054 leaving Granton-on-Spey with the 2.55pm train from Craigellachie to Boat of Garten in September 1957. Along with No 78053 this locomotive was to spend 4½ years allocated to Keith, working local services on the ex-Great North of Scotland lines, but it would ultimately be withdrawn from Bathgate, in December 1965.
W. J. V. Anderson / Rail Archive Stephenson

Above right:

Tillynaught, on the ex-GNSR coast line from Cairnie Junction to Elgin, was the junction for the Banff branch. Pictured on 11 June 1959, the other Keith-allocated '78xxx', No 78053, makes ready to leave with the 6.10pm to Banff — once the porter has finished loading the brake van. Transferred to Aberdeen Ferryhill in June 1961, this locomotive would be withdrawn from Stirling, in July 1964.
Gavin Morrison

Right:

Headed by a well-cleaned No 78046, the 'Scottish Rambler No 4' railtour of 19 April 1965 calls at Colinton, west of Edinburgh on a one-time Caledonian line. By now allocated to Bathgate — although the buffer-beam still proclaims 'HAWICK' — the locomotive would end its career at St Margarets, in November 1966.
D. A. Idle

Right:
None of the '78xxx' class was ever allocated to the Southern Region, but Willesden's No 78038 was selected to work the Locomotive Club of Great Britain's 'Surrey Wanderer' railtour of 5 July 1964. Well turned out for the occasion, the locomotive is seen traversing the (then) rarely used spur linking Birkbeck (Spur Junction) with Norwood Junction, whilst *en route* from Beckenham Junction to Caterham. *Brian Stephenson / Rail Archive Stephenson*

On the Southern Region

Left:
No 78038 passes Wimbledon 'C' signalbox, whilst running between Shepperton and Wimbledon on 5 July 1964. *Brian Stephenson / Rail Archive Stephenson*

Right:
Another picture of the LCGB tour of 5 July 1964, this time leaving Crystal Palace Tunnel, between Tulse Hill and Beckenham Junction. *Brian Stephenson / Rail Archive Stephenson*

BR Standard 2-6-0s in Preservation

Above: Following withdrawal by BR in the late 1960s a number of Standard 2-6-0s languished at Barry scrapyard, whence they were eventually rescued for restoration on various preserved lines. This picture shows what '2MT' No 78022 looked like when it arrived on the Keighley & Worth Valley Railway on 11 June 1975.
Some 17 years were to pass before the locomotive was working again.
Gavin Morrison

Right:
No 78022's tender arrived the same day on a separate low-loader.
Gavin Morrison

Left:
Sadly no Class 3MT 2-6-0 ('77xxx') made it into preservation, but four of the '4MTs' — Nos 76017, 76077, 76079 and 76084 — did, of which Nos 76017 and 76079 returned to working order many years ago. No 76017 is resident on the Mid-Hants Railway, while No 76079, based on the East Lancashire Railway, travels the country. Here No 76017 makes an impressive sight as it emerges from a cutting just east of Alresford *en route* to Alton on the Mid-Hants line on 27 October 1984. *Gavin Morrison*

Left:
Another view of the same train leaving Ropley. *Gavin Morrison*

Bottom left:
After restoration No 76079 made its home on the East Lancashire Railway, on which it is shown passing through Burrs Cutting on 18 May 1991. *Gavin Morrison*

Above right:
Beautifully restored and doing what it was built to do (i.e. work branch-line trains), '2MT' No 78022 heads along the Worth Valley between Haworth and Oxenhope on 16 January 1994. *Gavin Morrison*

Below right:
No 78022 ready for duty in Haworth Yard on 19 April 1994, alongside Stanier Class 5 No 5305. *Gavin Morrison*

Above:
No 78022, newly fitted with Giesl oblong ejector, at Haworth shed, Keighley & Worth Valley Railway, on 16 July 1995. *Dr John Sagar*

Below:
No 76079 speeds along the Calder Valley at Hebden Bridge with the 'Pennine Way' special (Preston–Huddersfield–Preston) on 19 January 2002. *Dr John Sagar*